Amit Grinfeld

Echoes of war:

The six day war 50 years later

Translation: Blue Lion Language Services
Cover and Book design: Studio Lev Ari

Amit Grinfeld

Echoes of war:

The six day war 50 years later

The modern history of an old nation

*For my dear wife and for our dear children.
For my late Grandfather, who ran into the fire
and saved life, in the six day war.*

Table of Contents:

Introduction:

Fifty years have elapsed since the Six Day War, and it continues to impact the State of Israel and its neighbors as if the war just ended. The new/old Israel, which was resurrected only three generations ago, cannot be explained without addressing the Six Day War and its outcomes. Every significant event since, largely stems from those six fateful days.

As a tour guide who travels around Israel and explains its sights and history to people from around the world, I keep rehashing a discussion about the outcomes of that war. A war that happened fifty years ago. A war where 22,000 people lost their lives in six days and around 300,000 people fled their homes. This war changed the face of Israel and the entire Middle East.

I wrote this book for anyone interested in acquiring a basic understanding of the Six Day War. The book discusses the reasons for the war its main events and its immediate and long-tern consequences. I did not delve into great descriptive depth of each and every battle, even though during the process of preparing this text I was exposed to immense volumes of written and recorded material. If you are interested in expanding your knowledge, there are countless books on the topic you can consult. There are also scores of excellent websites containing a great deal of information. The Israeli archives and also written and recorded material available from the Arab side of the conflict complete the picture for the contemporary reader.

A difficult challenge I faced was keeping my writing neutral on such a complex and charged topic. I am a Jewish Israeli, tour guide, and a major in the IDF reserves. I love my country and believe in its right to exist in security and in peace. In the end, I believe I managed to maintain a reasonable degree of objectivity. Remember, dear readers, that there is no such thing as history - only his story.

Either way, I'm confident that this book will give you a concise and factual read. It will shed light on historical events that happened fifty years ago, and which reshaped the fate of Israel and the Middle East. Half a century later the Six Day War still resonates strongly.

Enjoy the read!

Amit Grinfeld, Moshav Kidron, Israel. June 2017.

CHAPTER 1:

Historical Background

The State of Israel, the new country for the Jewish people in their ancestral homeland, rose out of the blood and fire of the War of Independence. A war that was waged between the winter of 1947 and the spring of 1949. The UN Partition Plan, which recognized the idea of two states for two nations - one Jewish and the other Arab, did not come to fruition. A brutal civil war broke out between the Arab inhabitants of the land who refused to acknowledge any partition, and the Jewish settlement. The Jews defeated the Arabs despite their inferior numbers. This was because the Arabs were much less organized, determined, and united. The State of Israel's independence was announced in Tel Aviv when the British left in May 1948. However, the next day the war escalated when the Egyptian, Jordanian, Iraqi, Syrian, and Lebanese armies invaded. During the following months, Israel managed to hold its own in the difficult battles, and pushed the invaders back from many areas. Some of these areas were intended for Israel in the UN's Partition Plan. At the end of the war, 78% of the British Mandate territory, previously Palestine, became the State of Israel. This was a historical and dramatic victory for the young Jewish state. However, it was not a complete victory.

Syria conquered several small territories from Israel during the war. In exchange for the Syrians' withdrawal, Israel was forced, when the armistice was signed, to agree to demilitarize the territories that Syria evacuated. Jordan conquered Judea and Samaria (jointly called The West Bank of the Jordan River). It also conquered the crowning glory of the Holy Land - the Old City of Jerusalem, and the majority of East Jerusalem. At the end of the war, Egypt held a small territory on Israel's southern coastline. Numerous Arab refugees congregated in this area, which was called the Gaza Strip, after the largest city there.

6,000 Jews (1% of the population) and 13,000 Arabs were killed in the war. More than 700,000 Arabs became refugees. In the following years, more than 850,000 Jews fled their ancient homes in Arab lands, and immigrated to the State of Israel. The young country also welcomed hundreds of thousands of European Jews. These European Jews survived the Holocaust, which exterminated 6 million Jews.

**A Maabara – Israeli absorption camp
for Jewish immigrents**

The Israeli population increased 4-fold in a span of less than two decades. The tiny country was being impressively settled. Millions of acres of land became modern agricultural plots. Hundreds of new towns were built, some on the ruins of Arab villages that were destroyed in the war, and some in desert and border areas. A unique and vibrant society was created in Israel. All this despite numerous social hardships and the poverty of that period.

In order to contend with the overwhelming advantage of Arab manpower and resources, who continued with their hostilities against Israel, it was decided to establish a national army. A combination of a professional army with popular characteristics of a militia. An army based on mandatory conscription, including virtually volunteer service. The overwhelming majority of Israeli Jews - men and women, have been required to serve in the army since the state was established. Most of the men and some of the women continue to serve in reserve duty for many years after. In the event of war, Israel developed an effective reserve recruitment model that can increase its regular army 4-fold within the span of 48 hours, thus maximizing the quantity of available manpower.

The IDF - Israel Defense Forces - is the apple of Israeli society's eye. It has always been society's melting pot. Jews from 172 different countries returned to their historical homeland and serve in the IDF with equal rights and equal responsibilities. There are also many non-Jewish minorities that serve in the IDF. This is a well-formed army, one that fights for a clear and simple purpose - to ensure Israel's survival. It is trained mainly for attack, based on the Israeli realization that the country is so small that there is simply nowhere to retreat to. In its first twenty years, Israel did not seriously fortify its borders. in the event of war, the IDF was prepared to move the battles to enemy territory, away from the vulnerable civilian population. This was a young and confident army that protected an ancient and long-suffering nation. The greatest fear of all was of a "second round" with the Arab countries. The IDF called this option "all out" - an all out war between Israel and all its Arab neighbors and their allies. Israel knew with certainty that the "second round" was not a question of if but rather a question of when.

The world saw Israel as a wonder, a tiny country in a hostile and violent sea. In the Middle East, the path to choosing violence as a way to solve problems is short.

Since the War of Independence, Israel did not enjoy widespread peace on its borders. Hostile terrorist activity was routine. Hundreds of shootings, murders, and terrorist activities have troubled those living along the borders and sometimes inland as well.

A terror attack destroyed a house in Tel-mond, Israel, 1956.

Up until the Six Day War, Israel's land was only approximately 8000 square miles (smaller than the state of New Jersey). More than half of this land was desert. Israel does not have any natural resources except for the minerals from the Dead Sea (the natural gas discoveries in the Mediterranean Sea occurred only in recent years). The small country is highly dependent on the import of products, particularly crude oil and wheat. Its strategic location, between Asia and Africa, and very close to Europe, is very important. This location exposed the land to countless invasions and wars throughout its lengthy history. Israel has access to both the Mediterranean Sea and the Red Sea (which is connected to the Arabian Sea and from there to the Indian Ocean). This same location has positioned Israel deep in the heart of the hostile Arab world.

Israel's land borders were problematic. After the War of Independence in 1948, there were no peaceful borders. Only borders with enemy countries that had signed no more than ceasefire agreements. And the fighting never truly stopped: In the North - a hostile mountainous border with Lebanon. In the Northeast - the Syrian Golan Heights towered threateningly above the inhabitants of the Hula Valley, where the Jordan River flows, and above the Sea of Galilee. In the East - the hills of Judea and Samaria controlled by Jordan overlooked the Jezreel Valley, the narrow coast line (where the majority of the

Jewish population lives), West Jerusalem and the narrow corridor that leads to it, and the Northern Negev desert. The Egyptian border, mainly the Gaza Strip, threatened the heart of the country and the Negev from the South. Israel did not have any strategic depth, in other words, room to maneuver in the event of an invasion. The Arab threat of "drive the Jews into the sea" was palpable.

The Arab leaders used hate for Israel as a smokescreen to distract the masses from poverty, backwardness, and corruption. The wounded Arab pride and the desire to exact revenge on Israel for defeating the Arab armies on what previously used to be Arab land, was strong. The suffering of the Palestinian refugees who were left in a perpetual state of statelessness and backwardness was easily manipulated to acts of terrorism against Israel. Terrorism is an inexpensive weapon that is easy to use. States that support terrorism can blur their responsibility as its emissaries. So, young Israel suffered from guerilla warfare and terrorism on all its borders. IDF reprisal operations, mainly against military targets of Arab states, only fanned the flames.

The Suez Crisis / Sinai War

In 1956, Egypt was about to receive a massive shipment of modern Soviet weapons. This deal was a real threat to Israel. Under the leadership of the new and charismatic leader, Gamal Abdel Nasser, Palestinian terrorism from Gaza reached new heights of death and destruction. The height of hostilities was in 1956 when Egypt closed the Red Sea to Israeli sea vessels. The Egyptian army placed cannons that controlled the Straits of Tiran in the southern Gulf of Aqaba (Gulf of Eilat). This marine siege was *casus belli*, meaning "a case for war". This offensive incident occurred at the same time as Nasser's announcement of the nationalization of the Suez Canal, which infuriated the two veteran European superpowers - France and Britain, who wanted to protect their rights in the Canal. Israel took advantage of the opportunity and hatched a plan for a military attack on Egypt together with the angered Europeans. For the first and last time in its history, Israel fought with the active assistance of foreign armies: the British and the French. These countries wanted to capture the Suez Canal and forcibly annul President Nasser's nationalization.

Two Egyptian land cannons placed on islands in the Straits of Tiran. Captured by the IDF in 1956.

The Sinai War was a military success. Gaza and the Sinai Peninsula were conquered by Israel. The Egyptian army was hit hard, and Israel's Western allies easily conquered the Canal (after waiting for the IDF to defeat most of the Egyptian army). However, then, due to immense pressure from the United States and the Soviet Union, the British and the French were forced to capitulate. Israel was forced to vacate the Sinai and the Gaza Strip. In exchange, Egypt gave a commitment with guarantees from the UN and the United States to demilitarize the Peninsula and ensure freedom of movement in the Red Sea. A peacekeeping force was deployed in Sinai.

Nasser lost the battle but won the war. The Suez Canal became officially Egyptian, and France and Britain were expelled from it in disgrace. The Middle Eastern conflict showed the world that new superpowers now controlled global affairs. Israel could find solace in the quiet that prevailed on its southern border for the next 11 years. A quiet that was necessary for the continued establishment of the fledgling state.

Israeli paratroopers in the Sinai desert, 1956.

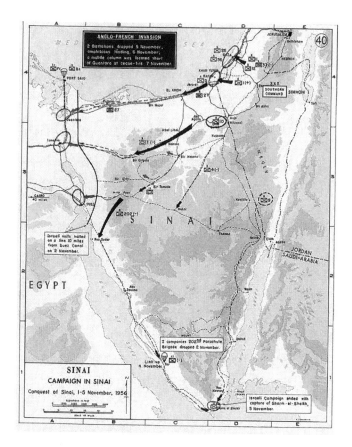

The main sequences of the Sinai War.

11 years later. The South is Quiet and the IDF Estimates a Low Probability of War

A decade after the Sinai War, the Israeli IDF Chief of Staff Yitzhak Rabin estimated that war with Egypt was not imminent. One of the main reasons for this estimation was the civil war in Yemen. Almost one third of the Egyptian army's fighting force, the largest of the Arab armies, fought with the royalists in Yemen. This war had no military victory and numerous casualties. These forces were sent there to promote Nasser's pan-Arab vision as leader of the modern Arab world. As long as Egypt's top forces were fighting far away from Israel, the IDF believed that Nasser would not want to get embroiled in a conflict with Israel as well.

Royalist soldiers in Yemen trying to push back an Egyptian attack with a recoilless gun.

The Jordanian Border

On the border with Jordan, mainly opposite Judea and Samaria and divided Jerusalem, Israel did not have peace and quiet. A long cycle of terrorism and reprisal operations became a bloody reality. However, the chances that the young Jordanian King Hussein would declare all-out war seemed slim. The Jordanian army - The Arab Legion, although professional, loyal and well-trained, was a small army intended mainly to protect the king's rule. Hussein ruled Jordan, a small and poverty-stricken country, using a supportive coalition of Bedouin tribes. However, the majority of the population was comprised of Palestinian Arabs, which created a constant challenge for the regime. Despite the local skirmishes with him, the king maintained a clandestine channel of communication with Israel. The hope was that if it was not possible to sign a peace treaty, there was a tacit understanding that neither side wanted to escalate the situation to war.

The Most Hostile Border of All

The border with Syria was almost constantly aflame. Syria was always Israel's most bitter enemy. It was the last to sign the ceasefire agreement and since 1948 the Syrians were relentless in their battle against Israel. They did this directly (via the military) and also indirectly (encouraging terrorism). The Syrians occasionally used force and sometimes hostile diplomacy. Remember that Israel was forced to agree to demilitarize several areas adjacent to the Syrian border. However, the agreement was up for interpretation, and Israel saw these areas as forbidden military zones but permitted for agricultural purposes. The Syrians, who claimed that no one was eligible to enter the zone, did not hesitate to shoot from the Golan Heights at anything moving in the demilitarized zones and often also outside these zones.

The residents in the Hula Valley, Ramat Korazim, and the Sea of Galilee suffered greatly from Syrian shelling and also from military raids and terrorism. Children's rooms were positioned inside the bomb shelters and the young people on these kibbutzim were called "the bomb shelter generation". The IDF's retaliations did not deter the Syrians, who made huge investments in building a strong fortifications line protected by immense minefields (the vast majority of which still exist and are lethal) that towered above the border with Israel. Despite suffering from political instability and numerous military coups, Syria maintained a close relationship with its largest patron - the Soviet Union. Of all the Arab countries, Syria was, and still is, the closest to Russia. Thus, the Israeli-Syrian border became a part of the Cold War. A conflict zone between the Soviet Union and the West, although the West's support of Israel at the time was much less direct than Soviet support of Syria.

The water issue was undoubtedly the culmination of the fighting between Israel and Syria. At first the Syrians, backed by the Arab League and the Soviets, tried to incorporate diplomatic pressure with shelling and bombing, to cause Israel to give up on working to divert the Jordan River, north of the Sea of Galilee, toward its National Water Carrier. Israel was in dire need of the Jordan River's water to irrigate central Israel and the arid northern Negev. The National Water Carrier of Israel was eventually built but it started on the shores of the Sea of Galilee, dug and protected inside a cave and with an enormous system of pumps that pumped the water from a height of minus 700 feet, to a height of more than 800 feet. In other words, because of the Syrians, Israel was forced to invest a great deal more time and money to build the national project.

The Syrians were still unhappy, and, prompted and funded by the Arab League, they started building a canal to divert the source of the Jordan River. The diversion canal was an extremely serious threat to 50% of Israel's main source of water. Furthermore, a sharp drop in the level of the Sea of Galilee would have caused the water in the lake to become overly saline. All of Israel's pleas at the UN to stop the Syrians were met with a Soviet veto. No other diplomatic tools were effective either. So, the IDF was deployed and it bombed the Syrian digging sites the digging equipment. The Syrians returned fire and between 1964 and 1967, these incidents culminated in days of battle with numerous casualties and much damage. Aerial combat, commando raids, tank and artillery fire were an everyday occurrence in the North, which only ceased subsequent to the Six Day War. The IDF, headed by then Chief of Staff Rabin, believed that all-out war with Syria was a realistic option and the Northern Command prepared and trained for the possibility of conquering the Golan.

The construction of the National Water Carrier, It was the
largest engineering project of Israel until today.

Chapter 2:

Dynamics of Overall Escalation, That No One Wanted

The Middle East ushered in 1967 with violence and tension. The Palestine Liberation Organization (PLO), which was created three years prior, developed into a serious nuisance for Israel. In 1965 it carried out 35 attacks on Israel. In 1966 it carried out 41 attacks. In the first six months of 1967, Israel had already been attacked 37 times. The aggressive reprisal operations that the IDF carried out against Jordan - the PLO's main delegation, lit the wrath of the people against the King of Jordan. Hussein tried to exhibit continued support for the fighting, but he feared war with Israel.

The Syrian border was constantly aflame. In early 1967, another military coup took place in Damascus (the fifth in less than twenty years) and the new and militant government wanted to cozy up even closer to the Soviet Union. On the seventh of April, the Israeli Air Force shot down 6 Syrian planes. Some were destroyed right over Damascus. The humiliated Syrians asked for Soviet assistance and the Soviets promised to send shipments of new weapons. Israel responded by announcing a large contract with the United States, which for the first time had begun supplying Israel with weapons. Although these deals did not come to fruition before the war, their announcement was enough to escalate the already tense atmosphere.

And then, in early May, the Egyptians and the Syrians received a false and fateful report from Soviet intelligence. It is still unclear whether this was a real mistake or an attempt by Russian officers to intentionally pour oil on the flames. Either way, they reported that large Israeli forces were gathering near the Syrian-Israeli border. Israel denied it and even invited the Russian ambassador to tour the area to see for himself that all was calm. But it was too late. Panic had been created and the Syrians quickly and publicly turned to Egypt for help since they had signed a mutual defense agreement.

Nasser found himself trapped between a rock and a hard place, in the spotlight. On the one hand, he did not want an extensive war and his military commanders admitted that the army was not prepared for a battle with Israel. Let us not forget that numerous Egyptian forces were engaged in battles in the Yemen desert. On the other hand, anyone who considered himself as leading the Arab world and the struggle against Israel could not sit idly by in case he was accused of cowardice. And so, the leader of the Arab world was led himself.

Once again, Nasser tried to manipulate the situation as best he could. The tension created an opportunity and excuse to gradually withdraw his forces from the mess in Yemen. He ordered his army to enter the Sinai peninsula. Concurrently, Nasser demanded from the UN that the peacekeeping force be evacuated and within days the blue helmeted soldiers disappeared. Now nothing stood between the IDF and the Egyptian army.

Nasser visits his pilots in an airbase in the Sinai, Days before the war

Nasser's great hope was to intimidate Israel into not attacking Syria, and extorting concessions on the demilitarization of Sinai from Israel and the superpowers. The threat of war without war. A sort of improved status before a future war at a more convenient time. His hope was that a new situation would be established where the Egyptian army was deployed, unrestricted, in the Peninsula and the Egyptian President's prestige would skyrocket. Nasser also believed that the Soviets actually supported aggression toward Israel.

Reports about violation of the Egyptian agreement were received in Israel that very same day - 5.15.1967. It was the Jewish state's 19th Independence Day and the IDF Chief of Staff was given an update on what was happening while watching a parade in Jerusalem. The government decided to carry out a general mobilization of the IDF. Within a few short hours, citizens from around the country were already starting to arrive at their reserve units. The small country began to gear up for war, which meant that the entire economy and all the resources were directed to the army. A general mobilization of the IDF increases the regular army by 4-fold, thanks to the reserves. However, there is a heavy economic and social price to pay and Israel, unlike the Arab states, could not keep all of its forces in active military service for long.

From the very start, the Israeli government asked to find a diplomatic way out of the escalating crisis. The moderate line was led mainly by the Prime Minister and Minister of Defense, Levi Eshkol. A smart and cautious man, which the public did not perceive to be a charismatic leader.

Eshkol tried to take action at the UN but the organization proved, once again, to be completely impotent. In any case the Russian veto torpedoed any potential move at the Security Council. Israel's patron and main arms supplier since 1948 - France, decided to turn its back on Israel and firmly demanded that Israel avoid initiating any military action. A French arms embargo was placed on Israel in its time of need.

Israelis donating blood, May 1967

Meanwhile, the crisis exacerbated. On May 23, Nasser decided to block the Straits of Tiran to Israeli sea traffic to and from the Eilat port. This action was again seen as *casus belli* - a case for war, according to international law. The mood on the Arab street was exhilarated and huge demonstrations in favor of a destructive war took over the urban streets. Overt calls were voiced in the Arab press and radio for the total annihilation of the Jews who had robbed Palestine.

The mood in Israel was quite different. The IDF was equipped and trained and the morale of the troops was high, but there was an atmosphere of fear and depression among civilians. The fresh memory of the Holocaust was enough to elicit existential fear. There was not much faith in the Prime Minister, who was perceived as a hesitant Diaspora Jew. The Israeli economy was paralyzed due to the general mobilization and everywhere people were digging defensive trenches, darkening lamps, donating blood, and other emergency activities.

In the final days of May, Eshkol continued to withstand the army's pressure to launch a preemptive strike and continued to seek external assistance. He turned to the United States, which had previously committed to assist in the event of an additional obstruction of the Straits of Tiran. However, the Americans were stuck deep in the mud of Vietnam and were afraid of another war breaking out with Soviet allies. They refused to help on their own and tried to recruit an international armada to open the sailing routes. Only Britain and Holland agreed to help and the attempt was a fiasco. Israel was left on its own.

Israel's only success was in securing America's understanding that Israel now had the right to use its army. It is important to note that in late May, the Russians became alarmed at the escalating dynamics that they contributed to. They tried to restrain the Arabs and pressure them not to attack first. Perhaps an Arab attack was indeed halted due to Soviet pressure. Either way, things got out of control. The immense pressure from the Arab street, demanding their leaders take action, was just as strong, perhaps even stronger, than restraining external factors.

At this point, many Israeli senior functionaries traveled to David Ben Gurion's lodge in the heart of the desert. They did it to seek good counsel and encouragement. The old legendary leader only warned that Israel should not initiate any action without the backing of at least one superpower. Particularly grave was Ben-Gurion's reprimand of the IDF Chief of Staff, Rabin. He accused him of imprudence and the desire to go to battle under inconvenient conditions and against a reasonable chance of tens of thousands of casualties. This had a very harsh effect on Rabin. Shortly after he collapsed under the pressure and was sent home for 36 hours. His deputy, Ezer Weitzman, managed to keep this from the public and the army and Rabin went back to functioning properly after he had rested.

The next grave event for Israel occurred on May 30. The King of Jordan could not longer sit idly while the streets were ablaze with calls for war with Israel. He signed a military alliance with Egypt and placed the Arab Legion under Egyptian command. Now Israel's worst nightmare was unfolding: a reasonable chance of all-out war in the North, in the East, and in the South.

**This Arab caricature shows Nasser kicking "The Jew"
out of Palestine.**

Jordan entering the ring heightened the pressure on Eshkol. The army required immediate action, first of all against the Egyptian army. Time was on Egypt's side, giving its army time to regroup and strengthen its forces in experienced units that started returning from Yemen. On the 1st of June, Eshkol was forced to capitulate to the demands inside and outside the political system and decided to expand his government. A direct outcome of the expanded government was the appointment of Moshe Dayan to the position of Minister of Defense. Dayan was a popular native born Israeli, bold, and aggressive IDF Chief of Staff in the Sinai War in 1956, who had already defeated Egypt in the past. He is considered the complete opposite of the drab and cautious Eshkol with the foreign accent. Him joining the government was perceived by the general public as an encouraging sign. Now there was another decisive voice in favor of launching a preemptive strike on the Arab armies.

Israeli civilians digging trenches

As stated, in early 1967 the heads of the Israeli security system believed that despite the tension and the violence - all-out war with Egypt and Jordan was not likely in the near future. However, escalation dynamics took over the Middle Eastern reality. Israel, Jordan, Egypt, the West, the Soviet Union, and even Syria did not want all-out war. However, after several turbulent weeks, in early June 1967,

Israel was surrounded by 3 armies of countries that were openly calling for its destruction. The Jewish state was in a panic, completely alone with its back against the wall, or more correctly, with its back against the Mediterranean Sea, where the Arabs were threatening to drive it. It was obvious that salvation would not come from the diplomatic front. It was also obvious to Israelis that time was on their enemies side, who were getting worked up in a frenzy of murderous propaganda. The general mobilization brought the Israeli economy to a grinding halt. A decision was then made to activate the full force of the Israel Defense Forces, in the air, on land, and at sea.

A table comparing Israel's forces to those of the Arab armies:

	Israel	Arab armies
Soldiers	264,000	547,000
Planes	300	957
Tanks	800	2500
Different types of ships	17	125

CHAPTER 3:

Operation Focus
(*Mivtza Moked*)

The Israeli government decided to go to war during a meeting it held on the 4th of June, 1967. The time was decided for the following day. The Six Day War was not a product of long-term strategic planning and Israel did not want to go to war in the first place. However, when the army was given a green light it was able to act according to early plans and to engage with a great degree of tactical freedom. According to these plans, the Air Force was activated first in order to try and crush the enemy's aerial power with a preemptive strike.

Israel had French-made fighter jets and bombers: Vautour, Mystere, Super Mystere, Ouragan, and Mirage III. The pilots were highly skilled and the ground teams were well trained. A plane could be fueled and armed within 7-8 minutes. The speed of preparing the planes for sorties greatly compensated for the numerical inferiority of 1:3 against the Arab air forces.

With much assistance from the Intelligence Corps, the Air Force prepared itself well for a preemptive strike. In planning the offensive operation, codenamed Focus, it was decided to focus first on destroying the enemy's runways. Thus, numerous planes would be grounded while those that did manage to take off would have no place to land. Israel, with France's cooperation, managed to develop special rockets that could blast deep holes in concrete runways. The Egyptian Air Force was chosen as the first target since it was the largest and most modern of the Arab air forces. It was decided to attack it with a maximum number of planes, while taking a risk that Israeli airspace would be virtually unprotected.

At 07:45 on June 5, it all began. When the Egyptian morning patrols returned for breakfast, and the base commanders were on their way to their offices, 200 Israeli planes appeared in Egyptian skies, which covertly took off and flew low to avoid radar detection. This was a rapid and dangerous flight. The planes did not come from the Israeli border but from the direction of the Mediterranean Sea and their arrival was perfectly timed so they would all appear at once above the Egyptian airfields.

It was a perfect surprise attack. The bombers first fired the new rockets that were developed against runways and rendered them useless, grounding hundreds of planes. Then, they began to fire on the parked planes, buildings and vehicles. The Egyptians sustained heavy damage on the first round - 197 planes were destroyed on the ground and another 8 in aerial combat. Additional Egyptian planes that managed to take off and survive the aerial battles crashed upon landing on the demolished runways when they ran out of fuel. In the second round of attack, another 107 planes were destroyed.

The third round of planes began choosing additional targets such as radar devices and electronic warfare equipment stations. All the planes attacked available targets like vehicle convoys. If we add Egyptian losses in the aerial battles, we will discover that within 4 hours, a total of 338 Egyptian planes were destroyed. These comprised 80% of the fighter jets and all the bombers. The Egyptian Air Force had been neutralized for the war, except for a number of courageous sorties. They bordered on suicide because of Israeli control of the sky. Most of the planes that survived did not make it to Israel during the war.

Egyptian jets that were Destroyed on the ground

An interesting story with immense impact in the war occurred above the military airfield adjacent to Cairo. Air Force planes identified a light Egyptian army transport plane that had just taken off. Since they were busy attacking the runways and fighter jets, the pilots decided not to intercept the light plane. General Abdel Hakim Amer, Commander of the Egyptian Army, was sitting in the light plane. He was shocked to the core by the sight of his air force being blown up on the ground and it led him to a decision, which we will get back to later.

At around 12:00, Syrian, Jordanian, and Iraqi planes began attacking targets in Israel. Some were downed by Israeli Mirages and they did not cause much damage. The Israeli response was quick and the fact that the Egyptian Air Force was already fatally wounded enabled Mordechai Hod, Commander of the Air Force, to now direct the air force to deal with the other enemies. In the following hours, the Syrian and Jordanian airfields as well as the H-3 Air Base in Iraq, were bombed. Although the Israelis did not benefit from the element of surprise this time, they managed to inflict heavy damage. Around half of the Syrian air force - 61 planes, were destroyed by nightfall, on the ground or in the air. The other Syrian planes flew far east - to Iraq, where they hid until the end of the war. The small Jordanian air force lost 29 planes and in essence ceased to exist. The Iraqis lost 23 planes and did not dare send more against Israel, except for a lone bomber on the second day of the war. That same bomber, by the way, did not inflict much damage with its bombs but it killed 14 soldiers when it was shot down by Israel and crashed directly on a military camp.

By the end of the first day of the war, Israel had managed to secure complete aerial superiority, which is extremely necessary in modern warfare. At a cost of losing 19 planes, the Israeli Air Force succeeded beyond all expectations. Four hundred and fifty one (451) Arab planes were destroyed - almost all of them on the ground. This was 47% of their air force. Since most of their other planes did not participate in any battles over the next five days, Israel took complete control of the skies.

A Mirage III plane, (now a monument), which took down 10 Egyptian planes during its service.

CHAPTER 4:

Sadin Adom (Red Sheet)

By Way of Deception

The IDF Chief of Staff Rabin directed most of the IDF's power southward. It was decided to attack the Egyptian enemy first. Egypt had 5 mechanized divisions and two armored divisions in Sinai at the time. Two Palestinian infantry brigades were deployed in the Gaza Strip. Moreover, in the evening of the IDF attack, there were additional experienced units in different stages of transit from Yemen to Sinai. The Egyptian army wanted to regroup in the heart of Sinai in order to keep a certain distance from Israel. A distance that would give them time to react in the case of an Israeli offensive. However the politics overtook military logic. Nasser commanded the army to deploy along the border to increase the threat to Israel. Since the escalation caught the Egyptians unprepared, their army had several serious problems:

1. A shortage of trained manpower.

2. Because of the demilitarization agreement, there were no defense systems ready in Sinai. Nevertheless, the Egyptians did manage to fortify several areas and plant minefields.

3. The Egyptian army was in the process of implementing Soviet doctrine, which it had not managed to complete. This fact contributed to the confusion and lack of coordination between the various units.

4. According to said Soviet doctrine, three formations must be deployed along the front. A patrol and warning formation, a central defense formation, and a reserve formation. The Egyptians only deployed the front formation. Their central defense formation barely had any trenches or concrete bunkers. Moreover, the Soviet doctrine relies on huge and continuous masses of army forces. Egypt did not have enough units, despite the size of its army, in order to create continuous lines of defense.

Although despite all its shortcomings, it was still a large army. The Egyptians concentrated around 1000 Soviet tanks in Sinai, and hundreds of cannons. It was a serious threat.

The Southern Command of the IDF had only around 450 capable tanks comprised of a mix of French light AMX-13 tanks, British Centurion tanks, old and trusty Shermans (with an improved Israeli cannon) and two new battalions of M48 Patton tanks from the United States. The two armies concentrated mainly on the northern part of the border, where the terrain was better for mechanized warfare. The forces of Yeshayahu (Shayke) Gabish, GOC Southern Command, performed an act of deception. Around one hundred and fifty administrative vehicles and recruited civilian vehicles were "dressed up" as tanks and armored personnel carriers. They used cardboard and wood for the job.

Just wood: A fake Israeli tank.

This large deceptive force moved from the army concentrations in the north of the Egyptian border. It was done while ensuring overt and noisy transit, to ensure that the Egyptians saw and heard. Even the Mossad assisted and activated double agents that would report the movement. The deceptive force reached the quiet border area near Kuntillah. Kuntillah is one hundred miles south of the area where the army was planning to invade. This phantom unit deployed camouflage nets and tents. A handful of real tanks joined the unit, which drove demonstratively and left clear tracks adjacent to the border. The Egyptians took the bait. They repositioned around three hundred tanks for redeployment against the phantom force. So almost a third of the Egyptian Armored Corps, along with the infantry and additional units, were lured away from the real battlefield. This entire force was not going to participate in the battles at all. Defenses of the area chosen for the IDF's offensive were diminished.

"Move!"

The order to attack Egypt, codenamed "Sadin Adom" (Red Sheet) was given at 07:45 on the morning of June 5. At the exact same time, the IAF's Operation Focus began. The IDF's communication networks sprang to life. Along the front, the camouflage nets were cast off and the engines started. It was decided to conduct the attack exactly half an hour after the first aerial attack conducted. That insured that the Air Force would be able to act with complete surprise, but when the ground attack would start, the Egyptians would not be able to regroup in time.

IDF Armored Corps soldiers mounting Centurion tanks.

The Southern Command assigned three armored divisions and two independent mechanized brigades to the battle. The artillery preparation was short and highly focused. The main emphasis was placed on the shock and speed of the maneuvering tanks and mechanized forces. The IDF relied heavily on the improvisational skill of the junior commanders and the soldiers' high level of training and motivation. It was fighting an army that relied on strict discipline and fear of the officers. The Egyptian army was large but had a slow and inefficient command. The IDF compensated for its numerical inferiority in soldiers and equipment with initiative, rapid attainment of a local advantage and determination.

The Israeli plan was divided into three main stages:

1. Breaking the front and opening passes for 4 armored brigades.

2. Flanking the main Egyptian forces deep in the Sinai and rapidly moving to their rear.

3. Completing the encirclement deep in Sinai and destroying the enemy forces when they attempted to withdraw and encounter Israeli forces behind it, who will capture convenient areas.

Much of the filed communications was done by female soldiers.
(The right one was taken by Kutin Assaf)

Although half an hour had passed since the bombing of the airfields began, the Egyptian communications channels failed to send warning to the frontline units. In several frontal outposts, the Israelis burst through with such surprise that they found Egyptian units in the middle of their morning inspections. The order to break through quickly created a situation where, at several crossroads of combat, the forces moved so quickly that they couldn't complete their mopping-up and forces needed to be assigned to eliminate pockets of resistance later on. By the evening of the first day of the war, the first line of the Egyptian front had been breached and the path to an offensive deep in Sinai had been opened. In the Gaza Strip, the attacking forces encountered bitter fighting of the two Palestinian brigades.

The ground forces received almost no help from the air because the Air Force was busy attacking the Syrians, Jordanians, and Iraqis. However, Fouga Magister jets were activated. The Fouga was the IAF's training aircraft. Armed with rockets and machine guns they served as flying artillery for the Southern Command against Egyptian positions, especially in the Gaza area. They were flown by pilot cadets or retired pilots who volunteered for the mission.

A destroyed Egyptian tank near Rafa (south Gaza strip).

Israeli infantry moving into the Sinai desert.

The Battle of Um-Katef Compound

The battle of Um-Katef, which began just after nightfall of the first day of the war was undoubtedly, decisive one. The Um-Katef compound was manned by 8,000 soldiers from the Second Egyptian Division. It was the largest compound that protected the Abu-Ageila junction area. A critical junction for the passage of forces into Sinai. The Egyptians were well entrenched, and protected by minefields and natural quicksand dunes that made movement difficult. They had tanks, tank destroyers, anti-tank guns, anti-aircraft guns and six whole artillery battalions at the rear of the compound.

The attacking force belonged to the division of General Ariel Sharon and included 14,000 soldiers, with artillery and engineering forces. The force had just spent an exhausting day in combat but was ordered to keep going. Sharon operated his forces impeccably. Two paratrooper battalions landed in helicopters to the rear of the Egyptians and attacked the artillery batteries, so that the Egyptian cover fire was sparse from the onset of battle. Israeli artillery, on the other hand, advanced to the front line, and from there it rained a curtain of fire. The Engineering Corps, at great risk, managed to break through breaches in the minefields. Infantry soldiers stormed the defensive trenches and conducted face-to-face combat using bayonets and commando knives. The Israeli tanks broke out of the wing, even before the battles in the trenches had ended, and penetrated the center of the compound. Close quarters battles were fought there against the Egyptian tanks. By sunrise, the entire large compound had been conquered. Thirty five (35) IDF soldiers were killed in battle. Dozens were injured. The Egyptian losses are unclear but it is clear that the large Egyptian force that protected the compound had been eliminated and its soldiers killed, injured, captured or escaped. The IDF expertly operated the principles of integrated battle, where different types of units cooperate. To date, the battle is studied by armies worldwide.

As soon as the fighting ended, Sharon's soldiers were not allowed to rest. They were sent to clear the traffic routes that the Um Katef compound protected. Other compounds were also conquered during the night. By early morning, large IDF forces from General Yaffe's division were already passing through the junction while maintaining exemplary order and without incidents of friendly fire. These forces broke through to the direction of central Sinai and staved off an Egyptian attempted counterattack on Abu-Ageila.

The Tal Division Breaks Through the Northern Axis

The division of General Israel Tal, considered a key figure in the Israeli Armored Corps, attacked the Egyptians through Rafah in the Gaza Strip. After the tanks passed through Rafah, they turned westward and engaged in fierce battles in the Jiradi compound, which was the fortified compound that guarded the road from Gaza to the town of El-Arish. The compound had 6.5 miles of defensive trenches, bunkers, entrenched cannons, and tank positions. By the afternoon of the second day of the war, after two offensives that did not succeed in eliminating the defense, the entire compound was conquered by the infantry and armored forces that were concentrated by General Tal. Shortly thereafter, the town of El-Arish was conquered. A successful 12-hour tank battle against the defenders and Egyptian reinforcements promised the IDF's takeover of the area. With the fall of the Jiradi compound and the Abu-Ageila junction two critical holes were created on the Egyptian front.

Two Fateful Orders

At 16:30 on June 6, General Amer who, if you recall, witness the destruction of Cairo's military airfield, made a fateful decision. He and his staff were shocked by the destruction of the air force and the fall of the large defense compounds on the front. Even though the majority of his army had not yet been hit, and large parts of it had not even gone to battle yet, he issued a general order to retreat. All of the Egyptian units were commanded to move westward as quickly as possible and to cross the Suez Canal to the African side. The message from his headquarters was immediately intercepted by Israeli intelligence, translated, and sent to the front within minutes. Gavish, commander of the Southern Command, was thus informed that the enemy would not fight for its positions. Moreover, he knew this before the Egyptians did. After consulting with the commanders of his divisions, he gave an order to storm westward. The troops were ordered not to dwell on pockets of Egyptian resistance but to bypass them. In essence, the IDF started chasing after the Egyptian army even before they had begun their escape.

Both of these orders, Amer's and Gavish's, sealed the fate of the war in the South and essentially the fate of the entire war. A critical race to the Canal had begun. The Egyptians tried to escape, the Israelis wanted to close the narrow mountain passes on the way West, in order to encircle and destroy the Egyptian army.

Two of the Generals of the south command: in the Right: General Gavish, commander of the southern front. On the left: General Sharon commander of the 38th division.

The Third Day — The Egyptian Army Falls Apart

The Egyptian army started to crumble and on the third day of the war it began to break apart as an organized force. Incoherent orders were given. The Egyptian command centers lost their ability to organize the battlefield. The long lines of retreating forces were an easy target for the Israeli Air Force. The bombers and the warplanes caused tremendous damage as they swooped down from the sky, shooting with whatever they had: machine guns, cannons, bombs, napalm bombs... The small number of roads in the Sinai and the large number of dunes and rocks around them, made it difficult for the Egyptians to spread out. There was little escape from the bombed traffic routes.

In the meantime, the first Israeli tanks managed to reach the mountain passes deep in Sinai. They were in such a hurry that some of the tanks ran out of fuel and other tanks towed them so that they would fight to block the roads. They succeeded in the mission and reached the crossings before most of the Egyptian units. The Israeli tanks fired at the slow lines of Egyptians and together with the Air Force created a situation where hundreds of weapons of war - tanks, armored personnel carriers, trucks, artillery and jeeps - were turned into target practice. They were trapped on narrow routes under fire from the ground and air, and with very low morale. Many of the vehicles that were not hit were abandoned by their teams, who escaped on foot into the relative safety of the desert.

The Israeli trap closed in. The Egyptian army was encircled deep in Sinai, confused, alarmed, and despaired. The large Egyptian force that was sent on the evening of the war to face off the IDF's phantom force at Kuntillah, also received an order to retreat. This force's tanks did not fire even one shell in the war and many were abandoned and captured by the IDF. In Kuntillah entire units fell apart once their commanders hurried westward without a fight, leaving their soldiers behind.

Not all the battles were so one-sided. In many cases, fragments of Egyptian units, and sometimes entire frameworks, fought back. There were many cases where the advancing Israelis were fired at from the dunes and from behind rocks. Also the Egyptian Air Force sent several sorties that were essentially on a suicide mission, seeing as the Israelis were in control of the skies. However, these ambushes and bombings did not manage to truly hinder the IDF or incur heavy losses.

On the third night of the war, a night parking lot for AMX-13 light tanks was suddenly attacked by an Egyptian tank force. The light tanks were completely inferior in protection compared to their adversaries-modern Soviet tanks, and they did not have night vision devices either. The light cannons failed to penetrate the Egyptian armor. By the time reinforcements arrived, the attacking forces had retreated. This IDF failure, in a very successful war for Israel on the whole, resulted in the light tanks being retired from service shortly after the war.

The Race to the Canal Ends

On the morning of June 8, the IDF's advance units arrived on the banks of the Suez Canal. By evening, the Israelis had already deployed along a new front line, on the water. Only one hundred out of a thousand Egyptian tanks managed to safely cross to the African side. The vast majority of their equipment was destroyed or captured in Sinai. The Egyptian army lost its fighting capability. Nasser was forced to ask for an immediate ceasefire, and the war in the South came to an end. That day, he announced his resignation as President of Egypt because of the enormity of the failure. Yet once again, Nasser managed to survive a military defeat. Massive demonstrations throughout Egypt over the following days, protesting the popular leader's resignation, made him change his mind. Nasser also contacted the King of Jordan. The Jordanians had also been defeated by that time and both leaders tried to coordinate versions. They decided to jointly blame the United States and Britain for helping Israel with aircraft carriers. Israeli intelligence intercepted the conversation and passed it on to the Americans and the British, who prepared a scathing diplomatic response. This added embarrassment to the resounding failure of the two Arab leaders.

**Israeli navy ship patrols the straits of Tiran
(Picture by Yaakov Agor).**

The leftovers of a routed Egyptian army unit.

In the days following the end of the war Egyptian soldiers continued to meander toward the Canal. Around 15,000 Egyptian soldiers were killed. Many of them simply died of thirst in the desert. More than 5,000 were captured. There were so many POWs that the IDF received an order to simply let the broken and unarmed soldiers cross the Canal. In several cases, some were shot as traitors by their own forces from the African side, while they were swimming across.

Brief Summary

The southern front in the Six Day War concentrated more than half of the IDF forces. They fought against the largest Arab army. It was won quickly using a tactic similar to that used by the Germans during their victories in World War II. It was Blitzkrieg - a lightning-fast war. After an air strike on the Egyptian planes, an armored and mechanized maneuver was made into the field. Penetrations were along selected axes in a concentrated manner, rather than against a wide front. All while managing an integrated battle with different types of units. The IDF commanders received intelligence and use it while on the move. The Israelis demonstrated improvisational ability, a high level of training, and tactical flexibility on the ground. The courage of the soldiers and junior commanders who believed in themselves was also salient. They knew that failing in the war could mean complete annihilation of everything they knew. Coupled with the generals' professionalism and leadership skills, the IDF was a brutal war machine.

In contrast, the Egyptian army lacked a fighting spirit. The quality of some of its corps was very low, and thousands of its soldiers were ignorant peasants forced to fill the ranks in the days before the war. They were never properly trained. Furthermore, the Egyptians did not manage to operate large frameworks of their quality units - which they had. These were well trained units with advanced equipment. The lines of defense were not properly prepared and many units did not take advantage of the days before the war for adequate entrenchment. The Egyptian logistic layout did not function professionally. The supply lines to some of the units were faulty even before the fighting began.

When the war broke out, Egyptian commanders lost their cool very quickly. Above all, General Amer's order for a retreat created a disorderly stampede. In fact, in the evening of the first day of the war, IDF Chief of Staff Rabin felt confident enough to transfer an entire paratrooper brigade from the reserves of the Southern Command to the fighting in Jerusalem. In the next three days, other forces were also transferred from the southern front to the north. They were transported hundreds of kilometers (Israel's not that small after all) in an impressive logistic operation in the final part of the brief war, and fought the Syrians in the north. The Egyptian defeat made it possible for Israel to win the war.

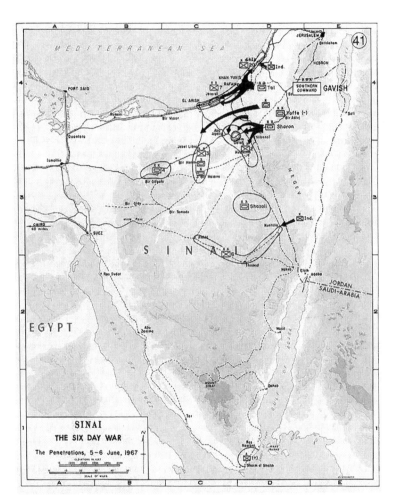

Israeli maneuvers of the 5ᵗʰ-6ᵗʰ of June.

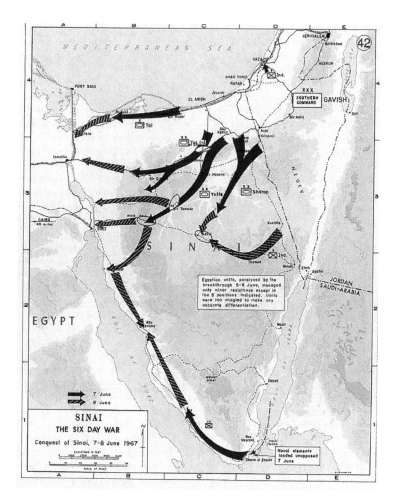

Israeli Maneuvers of the 7th-8th of June

Friendly Fire: The Liberty Incident

On June 8, just before the battles in Sinai ended, a very grave incident occurred in the Mediterranean Sea. The American technical research ship, the USS Liberty, was sailing not far from the shores of the Sinai Peninsula. It was attacked by Israeli planes and then by torpedo ships as well. The Liberty was severely damaged and almost drowned. Thirty four American sailors were killed. Israel later compensated the families with money.

Was this a series of mistakes? Mistaken identity? A coordination failure between allies? Or perhaps only some of the conspiracy theories that deny the version that claims that this was a mistake are true? Apparently there is no clear answer that everyone will find convincing.

Heavy demerge on the USS liberty after the incident.

CHAPTER 5:

The West Bank and the Holy City: The War with the Jordanians

"Israel has no intention of attacking Jordan"

When the fighting with the Egyptians began, Israel quickly sent a diplomatic message to the King of Jordan. Even before the war, Hussein was assured, in secret meetings, that Israel had no intention of attacking Jordan. The message was simple: If the Arab Legion does not open fire, Israel will also hold its fire. But the King decided otherwise. Young Hussein feared that if he instructed his army to not get involved in the war, a revolt would break out against him in Jordan. Also, he was committed to Egypt in a defense alliance, which he signed at the end of May.

Hussein and Nasser Signing the defense alliance

This alliance placed the Arab Legion under general Egyptian command. As soon as the battles began, the Egyptians encouraged the Jordanians to join what they called 'their victory'. Anyone who helps can split the bounty. They boasted that most of the Israeli Air Force had been wiped out, while the exact opposite was true. Did the Egyptians lie to the King on purpose or had they not yet realized the severity of the situation? There is no clear answer to this and the truth is probably somewhere in the middle. What is certain is that Hussein decided to join the war.

The Jordanians deployed nine infantry brigades in the West Bank, most of them in Samaria and Jerusalem. Two armored brigades equipped with modern American Patton tanks were parked near Jericho. They were considered the Legion's main reserve card. The Iraqi army sent an expeditionary force to help the Jordanians. When the war started one of its brigades was deployed near the Jordan river bridges, ready to enter its west bank. Three more brigades were on their way. The Egyptian army sent two Special Forces commando battalions, which were stationed in Amman. Although the reinforced Jordanian army was much smaller than the Egyptian army in Sinai, it had its own advantages:

1. It was a properly trained army and equipped with Western arms.

2. Its forces were deployed comfortably along prepared positions, unlike the Egyptians, who entered the demilitarized zone and did not have much time to entrench.

3. It held hilltops and mountains of the West Bank where there was good visibility and firing control on the lower Israeli areas. The height advantage gave the Jordanians more protection. Armored maneuver in the West Bank is limited to mountainous routes, and unlike Sinai, there were many settlements, some large and crowded. Harder area for armor maneuvers.

4. The Jordanian forces were adjacent to the Israeli capital and were deployed in positions that could have created an immediate threat to the coastal cities. The Jordanians were even able to rapidly cut Israel in two, and in some places the distance between their

forces and the Mediterranean coast did not exceed eight and a half miles.

In contrast to the Jordanians, the IDF Central Command did not have a large number of forces. Its units along Judea and Samaria barely managed to conduct a defensive battle. The armored reserve - the 10th Harel Brigade was kept in the Jerusalem Corridor. The urban line of the actual city was populated by a large infantry brigade, mostly comprised of the city's residents.

Initial Battles

At 09:40 on the morning of June 5, Jordanian soldiers opened fire with light weapons in various areas of the urban line in Jerusalem. Around twenty minutes later, cannons and mortars joined in fire. Neighborhoods and army bases were bombed in West Jerusalem and in the narrow Israeli corridor leading to it. Industrial facilities and civilian targets on the coast were also targeted, as was the Ramat David Air Force base in the Jezreel Valley and surrounding towns. Dozens of Israelis, soldiers and civilians, were killed or injured, and much damage to property was caused. Among other things, the Knesset building, the Israeli parliament, whose construction was completed only a year earlier, the Israel Museum, and the President's Residence were damaged.

Despite this, the Israelis were still attempting not to escalate matters and respond with force. In the first few hours, the Israeli Foreign Minister, Abba Eban, claimed that Jordanian fire was mainly a symbolic gesture of assistance to Egypt. A show that would soon stop. However, at midday there were reports of Jordanian air strikes and land movement: the Jordanians entered the UN neutral zone at Armon Hanatziv in Jerusalem, which posed a threat to the southern part of the city. So the government instructed the IDF to engage.

The Air Force, which had just finished dealing with the Egyptian aerial threat, began attacking the Jordanian airfields. This time, the Israeli pilots did not benefit from the element of surprise and encountered anti-aircraft fire and fighter jets. But this was not sufficient resistance. The small Jordanian Air Force was crushed within a few hours and completely destroyed. Israeli control of the Jordanian front's skies helped a great deal in the war, and mainly hindered and harmed the movement of the King's two armored brigades. It also offset the Israelis' relative numerical inferiority in manpower on the first day, since the majority of the IDF was fighting in the south.

The attack on Jordan begins

In the afternoon of June 5, Israel launched a ground attack on the West Bank. First in the Jerusalem area. The

Jerusalem Brigade - a reserve infantry brigade composed mostly of the city's residents, who saw their homes being shelled - acted first. They conquered Armon Hanatziv (the UN complex) and several outposts in the south of the city from the Jordanians. The Israelis had already trained to conquer these compounds.

In the Jerusalem Corridor there was an armored brigade equipped with Super Sherman tanks. Old tanks that were upgraded by Israel. In the war, these tanks proved that with trained and determined teams they could defeat modern tanks as well. The brigade began attacking northward, and pushed back the Arab Legion in difficult battles. After breaking through the strong line of outposts that threatened the northern Corridor, the tanks turned east. By the evening of June 5th, they had already reached the northern outskirts of Jerusalem.

**A super Sherman tank and half trucks of the 10th
in the Jerusalem corridor**

At the same time, the soldiers of the Jerusalem Brigade succeeded in conquering the Jordanian fortifications in the southern part of the city. They used a new weapon that was secretly prepared and placed before the war against the Jordanian positions. It was a double-headed rocket fired at the armed concrete walls of the Arab Legion. A small hollow bomb at the tip of the rocket blew a hole through the fort. Then, pushed by the force of the rocket's engine, a 5.5 kilogram TNT bomb entered forcefully. The second explosion that took place within the space created by the first bomb. This explosion was eight times stronger due to the fact that it was actually created within the enemy's fortification. In other words, it was equivalent to a blast from 44 kg of TNT. No Jordanian post survived such a hit. Once the bunkers were eliminated, the fighters could easily attack the connecting trenches and conquer them.

Within a few hours of battle, an Israeli threat was created on the divided city center and on the Old City in its heart. In the evening, the tough reserve paratroopers of the 55th Brigade arrived. The brigade was well equipped, but for desert warfare. Remember that this brigade was assigned to the Southern Command reserve and transferred to Jerusalem when it was clear that the Egyptians were beaten. It was an impressive logistic operation. Within a span of 12 hours, thousands of soldiers were moved from the Egyptian border to battle the Jordanians. The paratroopers were about to enter the most famous event of the Six Day War – the battle for the Old City.

The Ammunition Hill

After several hours of artillery fire and air strikes against the Jordanian artillery and mortar positions, an Israeli night offensive began on the heart of East Jerusalem. The Paratroopers were forced to grapple with a line of fortifications within an urban space. They did so courageously and with a willingness to sacrifice. One of the strongest Jordanian compounds was on a hill known as the Ammunition hill.

The battle of Ammunition Hill has become a myth over the years, and the site still exists as a museum for visitors. Like many other heroic battles, sacrifice and heroism were required because of several tactical errors. Errors that are evident with the wisdom of hindsight. The biggest mistake was the fact that the soldiers were mostly engaged against a huge outpost. The air force or the tanks did not manifest in the battle. The paratroopers fought fiercely against a company of Jordanian Legionnaires. The latter swore to the King that they would fight to death, which they did. Conquering the outpost took four hours, with brutal fighting in the trenches and bunkers. Thirty six paratroopers and seventy Jordanian Legionnaires were killed. Of the attacking force (more than one hundred men), only seven paratroopers were left unscathed in battle. The rest were killed or injured.

The capture of Ammunition Hill and the center of the Jordanians' fortifications line led to an Israeli connection with the enclave of Mount Scopus on the afternoon of the second day of the war. During these hours, the IDF also fought in other parts of the city, conquering the American Colony compound, the cemetery near the walls of the Old City, and the Rockefeller Art Museum in the corner of the northeastern wall.

Despite the Air Force's efforts to attack Jordanian armored forces coming from the direction of Jericho, several dozen tanks managed to enter into battle against the IDF in northern Jerusalem. But they did not manage to stop the momentum of the attack. The Jordanian Armored Corps retreated after it was hit by the IDF Shermans, which captured the area north of Jerusalem before they did.

Conquering the Old City

The next IDF target was the Augusta Victoria Compound. This old hospital and church was built by the German Kaiser on the Mount of Olives. It rises above the Old City to the east. The attack was launched on the morning of June 7. The entire force of the Paratroopers Brigade was activated. After several hours of fighting, the Mount of Olives and the entire residential area north of the Old City had been conquered. Now, after some hesitation, the paratroopers were given permission to storm the Old City. After a bloody battle on the bridge crossing the Valley of Jehoshaphat (Kidron), the fighters climbed up to the Old City from the east.

**An Israeli Sherman during a night battle next
to the mountain of olives.**

Jerusalem has witnessed dozens of wars in its ancient
history. Almost all of the attacks on the city were on its
northern side, which is more convenient for a topographical
attack. The city had been conquered by Jews only twice.
Both times from the East. Once by King David 3,000 years
ago, and the second time by the Israeli paratroopers. The
commander of the Paratroopers Brigade, Mordechai
(Motta) Gur, broke through the ancient iron doors of
the Lions' Gate with his half track. Hundreds of his man
behind him.

By evening of the third day of the war, the Old City had
been mopped-up of the last of the Jordanian snipers. An
Israeli flag was hoisted on the Temple Mount and the
excited paratroopers rushed to touch the stones of the
Western Wall, the remnant of the Temple, and to say a
quick prayer. The famous sentence recorded from the
IDF's communications system "The Temple Mount is in
our hands" became one of the symbols of the war.

A tired paratrooper prays at the western wall

The Battle in Northern Samaria

On the afternoon of June 5, during the initial hours of the war, Jordanian artillery batteries were fired at an Air Force base near Kibbutz Ramat David in the Jezreel Valley. Several Jordanian Hawker-Hunter planes made sorties on targets in the Israeli home front. To eliminate this threat, forces from the IDF Northern Command were sent to attack northern Samaria in the Jenin area. The primary objective was to destroy the cannons. The force assigned to the attack was a division of infantry with support of Super Sherman tanks, centurion tanks and light AMX-13 tanks.

In the first hours of the battle, the IDF managed to break through the front line, reach the artillery positions, and neutralize them. British Long Tom guns, which were the most dangerous long-range artillery threat, were among the weapons captured. On the eve of the first day of fighting, Defense Minister Moshe Dayan decided to expand the scope of operations in Samaria. An order was given to conquer Jenin and clash with the Jordanians deeper in the area. Behind the order was the tactical logic of engaging numerous Jordanian forces away from the battles in Jerusalem. The result was the development of armored battles in the Dotan Valley area of Samaria.

A British-made Long-Tom cannon captured from the Jordanian army. Displayed at the Israel Defense Forces History Museum in Tel Aviv.

The Jordanian army defended the area with an infantry brigade reinforced by one tank battalion. On the second day of the war, Jordan's decorated elite, the 40th Armored Brigade, joined the fighting. All the Jordanian tanks were new American Patton tanks. The 40th Brigade entered into combat after a long drive from Jericho. Despite the Israeli Air Force attacks, this brigade did not sustain significant losses on the way. However, the arrival of the Jordanian Armored Corps only at dawn of the second day of the war, enabled the IDF to climb up from the Jezreel Valley and capture high areas. Therefore, the main battle for northern Samaria took place deep in the territory under conditions that were less favorable to the defenders.

It was the only big armored battle that took place on the Jordanian front. It lasted intermittently for 36 hours. Both sides suffered heavy losses, but the older Israeli tanks eventually won. The 40th Brigade of the Jordanian army was hit hard in battle. This unit did not break under the pressure of battle, and its forces did not escape in mayhem, but withdrew in a relatively orderly fashion.

The IDF lost 33 soldiers and dozens were injured in northern Samaria. 150 Jordanians were killed, hundreds injured and captured, and their tanks destroyed.

IDF infantry advance into a village in Samaria

When the pressure increased on the third day of the war, King Hussein of Jordan realized that the chances of protecting the West Bank were slim. East Jerusalem fell and it was clear that now the Israelis were free to attack Samaria from this direction as well. The King ordered a general withdrawal from the West Bank. The great achievement of Jordan's occupation from the 1948 war became a thing of the past. The majority of the Jordanian soldiers managed to disengage from the Israelis and retreat. But the losses to the tanks were great and only a few of them reached the Jordan Bridges. Many Jordanian soldiers, who were residents of the West Bank, deserted during the withdrawal and simply fled to their homes. Despite the harsh losses, the King managed to save most of his army. The Arab Legion was not destroyed like the Egyptian army. But the Jordanians were undoubtedly defeated and no longer posed a threat to Israel in the war.

Ceasefire with Jordan

In the morning of the fourth day of the war, the Egyptian and Jordanian forces were defeated. Hussein asked for a UN-brokered ceasefire. As mentioned before, Nasser called Hussein and asked him to join him on a campaign of false accusations against Britain and the United States.

**King Hussein announce of the lost
of the west bank.**

Brief summary

With its victory over Jordan, Israel had conquered territories in the heart of the country. The West Bank is much smaller than the Sinai, but it's mountains are critical to the army that wants to protect Jerusalem, Tel Aviv, and the populated heart of Israel - the coastal plain. There are also holy places in the West Bank, particularly the Temple Mount in the Old City. For the first time in almost 2,000 years, the Jewish people reigned in Judea and Samaria - the land of the Bible. This historical event has had an electrifying effect on Israeli society, the Jewish community, and large parts of the Christian world. Concurrently, the fall of the Islamic holy sites in Jerusalem under Israeli control shocked the Muslim world, especially the Arab world.

Refugees

The development of the Israeli offensive on the West Bank prompted a wave of panic among the hundreds of thousands of Palestinians living there. Part of the civilian population began to flee to Jordan - most of the escapees did so during the war and a few in the days that followed. The number of refugees the fled the West Bank to Jordan in 1967 is estimated to be around 180,000. Unlike the 1948 war, whose battles were slower, bloodier and more encompassing, the Six Day War did not involve the destruction of villages.

The exception was the strategic Latrun projection. Here the Jordanians fought off the IDF during the War of Independence time and time again, and many were killed. The area controlled the only road between Tel Aviv and Jerusalem at the time. Israel decided to destroy the 4 Arab villages there and expel their inhabitants. But overall, the overwhelming majority of the Arab population in the West Bank remained. A post-war census counted around 700,000 Arabs. All these were now under the Israeli government's responsibility.

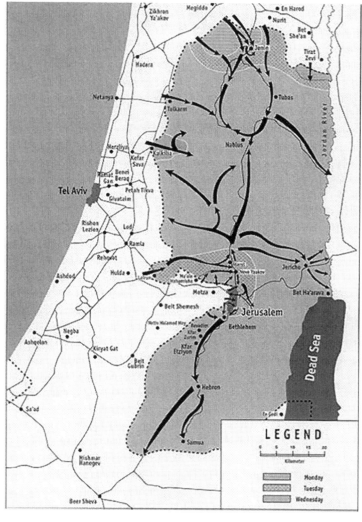

Map of the campaign in the west bank

CHAPTER 6:

Conquering the Golan Heights

From the early hours of the war, Syrian army artillery made a great deal of noise, which was heard by the Israeli communities at the foot of the Golan Heights. There was a lot of damage and several kibbutzim, such as Kibbutz Gadot, were completely destroyed. Two civilians and eight soldiers were killed, dozens injured. The relatively minor civilian losses were the product of many years of experience living under fire in the north. The women and children were immediately taken to the bomb shelters, and they were already very familiar with Syrian bombardments.

The forces that the IDF deployed in the North at the beginning of the war were for defense purposes alone. Remember that the majority of forces were concentrated on the Egyptian border and some at the Jordanian one. Northern Command units were found in a topographically inferior area - the Hula Valley, Ramat Korazim and the Kinneret Valley (the area around the Sea of Galilee). The Syrians held the basalt Golan Heights and built about thirty strong outposts along the border with Israel. The border between the two countries passed at the beginning of its lowlands, meaning that the Syrians had an elevation advantage.

Despite the lengthy rivalry, in the first days of the war the Syrian front was secondary to Israel. The IDF did not have enough forces to attack at this stage. Interestingly, the Syrian army did not deploy all of its forces in the Golan as well. Its units manned the bunkers and trenches of the defense lines built by the Soviets. But no heavy reinforcements were sent. Quite a few units remained deep in Syria, mainly near Damascus. Among them were the most loyal elite formations. The reason was the nature of the Syrian regime. It was a military regime with a history of repeated coups that sought first and foremost to protect itself from internal enemies. Israel was an external enemy to which hatred and propaganda were channeled to blow off steam. But it was not perceived as an existential threat.

Still, six infantry brigades, assisted by some 200-250 tanks, were deployed in the Golan Heights. Most of the Syrian tanks were old but there were also a few modern Soviet T-54 tanks. It was around half of the Syrian army's force.

Between the 5th and 8th of June, the Syrians were satisfied mainly with an artillery barrage. Two local attacks against Israeli Kibbutz communities were thwarted. The IDF responded with artillery fire. The Air Force, from the second day of the war, concentrated more than two-thirds of its air strikes on the Syrian defense lines. The Israeli bombings caused damage and losses. But it was not enough to neutralize the powerful bunkers that had been prepared for years. Most of the Syrian artillery continued to fire. The planes mainly caused psychological damage to the Syrian soldiers, which I will elaborate on later.

Israeli air attack on Syrian bunkers

Syrian planes did not take part in the war and left complete control of the skies to their adversaries. We must remember that the Syrian air force was badly hit on the first day and what remained of it took cover in Iraq, outside the range of the Israeli planes.

Hesitation

Even when it was already clear that the battle against Egypt and Jordan was developing in the right direction, Defense Minister Moshe Dayan hesitated to instruct the IDF to attack the Syrian lines on the Golan Heights. He feared that the huge minefields and the numerous well-dug outposts would turn an offensive on the Golan Heights into a bloody battle. Dayan expressed concern of about 20,000 casualties. However, he changed his mind, partly because of the immense pressure from the residents of the North who demanded that the Syrian nightmare be eliminated. The Northern Command's forces, which meanwhile received reinforcements from the Central Command and even from the Southern Command, wanted to play a more active role in the war. After all, Northern Command units, such as the regular Golani Brigade, had been training for the scenario of attacking the Golan Heights for years.

The Offensive

The offensive was launched in the early morning hours of June 9. The IDF concentrated a strong force for this battle: three infantry brigades, two mechanized brigades, one armored brigade, and one paratrooper brigade. In addition, parts of the 10th Armored Brigade and the 55th

Paratroopers Brigade, who had just finished fighting in Jerusalem, were also able to take part in the battles. The entire Air Force was instructed to help in the attack. This time, the IDF fought against only one army because the defeated Egyptians and Jordanians abandoned the Syrians in battle. This gave the IDF a numerical advantage, but it faced a well-fortified adversary in an area convenient for defense. It is also important to remember that of all the Arab countries, Syria benefited from the closest relationship with the Soviet Union. There was a concern that the superpower would diplomatically, and perhaps even militarily, intervene on behalf of the Syrians.

The Syrian army estimated that the IDF would try to break through the central border zone. There were several ancient roads in the area that had always led from the Land of Israel to Damascus. Therefore, the area was carefully guarded and many outposts protected the passages. However, the IDF chose to concentrate a blow in the northern Golan Heights. The few roads were somewhat compensated by the terrain: high slopes but not particularly mountainous so that trained tank crews could maneuver through them.

In order to confuse the Syrians, secondary attacks were also conducted in the south and center of the front. These attacks managed to conquer a narrow strip of about six miles from the Syrian front outposts in the middle of the Golan. In several places there the IDF fighters landed in helicopters directly on or behind the fortification lines. They did not always encounter resistance. An example was the Fik outpost in the southern Golan Heights. The soldiers landed with the helicopters and found many wounded Syrian soldiers in the outpost trenches. They found one soldier, sitting on an antiaircraft cannon, which could easily shoot down an approaching helicopter. The Syrian simply sat there with his eyes wide open, muttering the Arabic word "Tayirat", meaning planes, over and over again. This was a result of the shock of three days of bombings.

Although the IDF units did not deeply penetrate this area, the attack achieved its goal: much of the enemy's attention was concentrated in the wrong place.

Harsh Jordan Valley Battles in the Northern Golan

The young soldiers of the 1st infantry Brigade "Golani" were chosen to attack the strong Syrian outposts on the northern part of the border. In their southern wing, the 8th mechanized brigade attacked. First they stormed Tel Azzayat, which was a huge array of outposts that often fired down at the Israeli settlements. The locals called it "the monster on the hill". Golani soldiers, who had trained a great deal to attack the place, managed to capture the hill smoothly and with only one casualty. The speed of the attack and the correct maneuvering to the rear of the outpost while breaching the minefields, made it possible to effectively neutralize the Syrians.

Tel Faher

The next target was the Tel Faher outpost, which stood higher on the slopes of the Golan. Here the battle got complicated. Under the fire of machine guns, mortars, and artillery, the advancing battalion's battle plan was disrupted. Tanks from the aid battalion were hit, along with numerous half-tracks. The disrupted progress brought the fighters directly to the extermination area in front of the large outpost. An entire Syrian platoon was entrenched there, using a tank, mortars, an anti-tank gun and medium and heavy machine guns. Numerous soldiers were hit in attempts to rescue their injured comrades. The battalion commander sent one of his platoons to a dangerous frontal assault on the southern part of the outpost. They did it while sustaining losses. In a number of cases, soldiers lay on the barbed wire fences to allow their comrades to step on them and move ahead. In face-to-face combat, the soldiers managed to eliminate the defenders. The Israeli-made Uzi submachine gun, used by the Golani soldiers, greatly aided in the fighting in the narrow trenches. It was a weapon with strong firepower. Despite its limitations in accurate long-range shooting, the small Uzi was particularly lethal in face-to-face combat in the bunkers.

Syrian fortifications in Tel-Faher

However, the northern part of the Tel Faher outpost continued to fire in all directions. The battalion commander was killed there when he led the mop-up of a trench. Only the arrival of small forces to the rear of the outpost and their entering the trenches in face-to-face combat eventually led to an Israeli victory. After more than three hours of battle, at 18:15, Tel Faher was conquered. The attacking battalion lost 34 soldiers, including its commander, his deputy, and two of the battalion commanders. One hundred fighters were injured. Half of the force that left the Hula Valley in the morning offensive were lost by the evening.

Breaching the Syrian line

The tanks and armored personnel carriers of the 8th mechanized Brigade advanced slightly south of the Golani Brigade towards the outposts and villages of the Za'ura area. The Syrian outposts in front of them were conquered during heavy fighting. Most of the tanks that were hit that day sustained fire by anti-tank squads that dispersed among the houses of the Syrian villages. By evening, despite the heavy losses and damaged equipment, the brigade managed to advance deep inside the area.

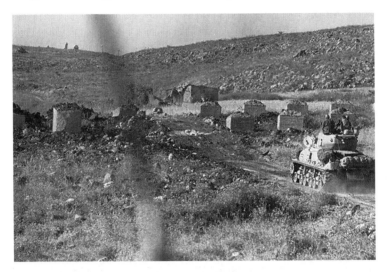

Israeli tanks moving up through Syrian road blocks

Because of the Israeli air force's complete control of the sky, the few reinforcements the Syrians sent to the front line that had been breached failed to move on the roads. Tanks and vehicle convoys discovered in the area were immediately bombed. The Israeli Air Force successfully isolated the battle zones.

At the end of a day of fighting on June 9, the Syrian line was breached in the northern Golan Heights after a tough battle. In the central Golan, and in the southern Golan, albeit damaged, the line was not completely conquered. At this time, the Security Council if the UN held heated discussions about a ceasefire. It was also clear that Russian interference might come at any moment. Meetings were also held in Jerusalem. Defense Minister Moshe Dayan claimed that it was necessary to stop and be satisfied with what had had been achieved up to that point. He was very concerned about Russian interference. Prime Minister Eshkol, who showed restraint on the eve of the war, ordered now to continue the conquest of the Golan Heights until the area of its capital, Kuneitra.

The Syrian Army collapse

During the night of June 9, the Syrian army was broken. Officers and commanders fled from the battlefield and entire ranks of soldiers followed suit. Outposts and weapons were abandoned. At the same time, the Damascus headquarters gave an official order to withdraw and prepare for the defense of the capital. But it was no longer relevant because the army had already fallen apart and escaped.

When the IDF's progress was resumed the next morning, it already faced almost zero resistance. At 08:30 in the morning, Damascus radio broadcasted a message that the town of Kuneitra had fallen. To this day, the reason for the announcement is unclear since the IDF had not yet reached the capital of the Golan Heights. This may have been an attempt to expedite the withdrawal or involve the Russians. What is certain is that it contributed to the panic and the Syrian army's flight. IDF forces advanced rapidly and by the afternoon, 60% of the Golan Heights had been conquered, including Kuneitra. The rest was left in Syria's possession.

IDF Artillery battery in the Hula valley.

At Kuneitra, IDF soldiers captured numerous documents from the Syrian army in an abandoned headquarters building. Among other things, maps of Syrian plans to conquer the Galilee, Jezreel Valley and Haifa Bay were discovered. The Battle for the Golan ended after 36 hours. At this stage of the battle, the government halted the IDF's advance for three reasons:

1. Achieving a 10-14 mile deep security zone in the Golan and the capture of the volcanic ridge in the heart of the Golan Heights is what gives Israel a height advantage to date.

2. Enormous diplomatic pressure from the Soviet Union and the United States to end the fighting, and the risk of actual Soviet intervention, which could deteriorate into a dangerous international conflict.

3. Israel had no desire to embark on a war of conquest and territorial gain in the North. Capturing the Golan was intended to secure the water sources and to distance the Syrian threat from the Galilee and the Sea of Galilee.

The Eight Day War

The ceasefire on June 10, 1967 is considered the end of the war. In fact, Israel's military activity did not end until June 12. Over the next two days after the battle, helicopters landed IDF ground forces on the peaks of the Dov Ridge and the high Hermon Mountain, which are north of the Golan Heights. These tall mountains (Israel actually conquered only 5% of the mighty Hermon Ridge) enabled the Syrians to set control of fire and lookout on northeastern Israel. Since it was a military occupation operation in every respect, even though there was no fighting there, it is possible to say that the Six Day War was actually an 8-day war. The capture of this range was the final military activity of the war.

Golan Heights Refugees

When the war started and the IDF began bombing and shelling the Golan Heights, a wave of refugees moved toward Damascus. In the two days of the Israeli ground offensive and in the weeks that followed, most of the residents of the Golan left their homes. The vast majority fled before the IDF reached their villages, but some were also expelled after the fighting ended. The exact numbers are not known, but up to 120,000 people left their homes. Exceptions were the residents of the four Druze villages of the northern Golan Heights who remained on their land with Israel's approval. Aside from them, none of the Syrians that lived in the Golan Heights on the eve of the war remained. These Syrians are not considered refugees today, because they have resettled in their country's territory. The land that Syria lost in the Six Day War comprises only 0.67% of its territory.

The map of the battle of the Golan Heights.

CHAPTER 7:

The War is over! What do we do now?

On the morning of the 5th of June 1967, Israel faced a real and clear existential threat. A week later, the three threatening Arab armies were badly beaten and unable to continue in the war. The IDF managed to conquer 23,552 square miles of the Sinai desert, 2,162 square miles of the West Bank, and 482 square miles of the Golan Heights. The total area that the IDF gained in six days was almost 3.3 times greater than Israel on the morning of June 5. Strategic depth was achieved for the purpose of defending Jerusalem, Tel Aviv, and other major population centers. The water sources in the North were secured. In the Sinai Desert and the Gulf of Suez, there are several oil wells that for a while produced about 75% of the fuel consumed in the Israeli market at the time. Thus, Israel also obtained energy independence.

Causalities of the war

	Israel	Arab Armies
Killed in Action	776	21,000
POW	15	5,462
Lost Aircraft	46	500+
Lost Tanks	Dozens (Many where later repaired)	Hundreds

Subsequent to the war, the Israelis opened the way to Bethlehem, Jericho, and Hebron, where the Cave of the Patriarchs (the grave of the patriarchs and matriarchs of the Jewish people) is located. The road opened to Nablus, Beit El, Shilo, Gaza... In the Golan Heights there are ancient synagogues alongside the ruins of the Jewish city of Gamla. The antiquities of Kursi, Banias, and many other sacred Jewish and Christian sites were now under Israeli control. Historical and archeological world heritage sites were now under Israeli control. Up until then these sites had been inside enemy territory and therefore completely inaccessible. However, most of the Israeli and global attention was given to Jerusalem.

On Temple mount. Rabin is one the right, Moshe Dayan and General Narkis – Commander of the central command in the middle.

Jerusalem... The Old City... The Temple Mount... Magical names and words for the Jewish people. The Old City of Jerusalem is deeply etched in the collective memory of the Jews. For generations, they swore "next year in Jerusalem" in their prayers. The Jew is commanded to pray facing the foundation stone at the top of the Temple Mount. This is where the First and Second Temples stood. The only physical place that is scared to all Jews. Think for a moment about what the contemporary Jewish national movement is called: "Zionism". And what is Zion? One of Jerusalem's ancient names. The return to the old holy Jerusalem is implied by the name of the Jewish national movement.

Indeed, rumors of the liberation of the ancient Jewish Quarter and the opening of the road to the Western Wall spread like wildfire throughout Israel. In the days following the war, hundreds of thousands of Israelis visited the holy site on the Temple Mount - the Western Wall, remains of the Temple. A wave of religious excitement washed over the young and victorious country. It didn't stop in Israel. Millions of Jews and hundreds of millions of Christians watched with astonishment as Jewish sovereignty over the Old City was restored.

Concurrently, the Muslim world was flooded with a sense of humiliation. Rage and vengeance erupted when the Dome of the Rock and the Al-Aqsa Mosque, the third most important in the Islamic world, fell into the hands of the Jews. The Temple Mount, *Haram al-Sharif* in Arabic, was under Muslim control (except for a brief Crusader period) for 14 centuries. The Jews, considered by Islam to be an inferior religion belonging to a small and weak group of despicable people, succeeded in "putting their filthy hands on an Islamic holy place." Not only did a group of Jews succeed in settling in Palestine - they now took over additional lands belonging to the "Nation of Islam". This disgrace will only be erased with re-conquest and revenge.

Knowing the feeling of Muslim humiliation, Moshe Dayan declared immediately after the war of Muslim autonomy on the Temple Mount. On the eve of the war, Dayan feared the conquest of the Old City because it was a political and religious time bomb. "What will I do with this Vatican?!" He was disgruntled on the eve of the attack in Jerusalem. Dayan grew up among Arabs and was very familiar with the Temple Mount's religious significance for Muslims. He ordered the Israeli flags to be removed a few hours after being placed there by the fighters.

Ever since, Israel had always treated the Temple Mount with extreme caution - as if it were a ticking bomb. Its security forces work very hard to identify anyone who tries to fan the flames around the Temple Mount. There is always a serious concern that extremists will try and sabotage the Muslim structures on the Temple Mount. Such an act could ignite a world war between the State of Israel and the entire Muslim world (which currently has nearly two billion people).

Praise

After the war, victory albums were printed praising the heroism of the soldiers and the genius of the leaders - Moshe Dayan, Yitzhak Rabin, and others. Blinded by victory and success, Israel looked proudly at the IDF and in subsequent years many were certain that after the great victory, the Arabs would not dare to fight again. And if they try, the IDF will easily crush them. The hundreds of Israeli casualties were buried as heroes who died for glory and triumph. Their deaths are seen as heroic and they are not treated as tragic victims like those of the War of Attrition or the Yom Kippur War, which took place several years later. The majority of Israelis have no idea how many soldiers the IDF lost in the Six Day War (close to 800). The glory masks the grief.

For most Israelis, the architects of the war's victory are undoubtedly Yitzhak Rabin, the IDF Chief of Staff, and Moshe Dayan, the Defense Minister. For years, Prime Minister Levi Eshkol was not perceived as the architect of victory. An injustice was done to him when the first history books were written on the subject. Eshkol died only a year and a half after the war, after two heart attacks. Perhaps the days awaiting the war and the days spent fighting sapped him of his remaining health. Only many years after the Six Day War did Israel begin to understand the man's greatness. Eshkol was a true diplomat. As a cautious prime minister, he tried to prevent war and bloodshed, but he also knew how to lead Israel in war and encouraged the security forces to carry out their duties.

One of the victory albums, printed shortly after the war.

Strength

The IDF did not stop growing or fighting in the wake of the war. The army grew in the coming years and acquired equipment that was more modern. It began to rely on American weapons. The United States began to see Israel as a small and tough ally in the heart of the Middle East. Skyhawk and Phantom planes, Hawk missiles, Patton tanks, and other equipment were purchased from the United States, which became Israel's main arms supplier. Thus, the assimilation of the Israeli-Arab conflict intensified within the Great Cold War conflict. In the seven years that passed until the Yom Kippur War, the IDF almost doubled in size.

Alongside the continued military buildup of the IDF, there is a salient conceptual change in Israeli society and leadership: no longer a threatened and frightened society but a society with proven military strength. These perceptions led an Israel, blinded with excessive self-confidence, to the surprise at the outbreak of the October 1973 war. Although the IDF was certainly not defeated in this war, the Israeli public lost its blind trust in the leadership.

"The Territories" as a Bargaining Chip for Peace

After the war, there was a widespread perception in Israel that it would now be possible to make peace with the Arab world. The young country finally had an important bargaining chip with the Arab countries: "the territories". The territories occupied in the war were - the Golan Heights from Syria, Judea and Samaria from Jordan, the Gaza Strip and the Sinai Peninsula from Egypt. No real negotiations were held with Arab countries before the war. The Arabs demanded Israel's very existence be revoked. But the rules of the game changed abruptly in 1967. Many hoped that a permanent peace treaty could be reached with the Arab states by returning all or part of the territories captured in the war.

The great diplomat, Israel's Foreign Minister Abba Eban, worked tirelessly at the UN to help formulate UN Resolution 242, which is a roadmap for achieving peace on the basis of returning territories captured in the war. In short: Land for peace. To this very day, this decision constitutes the UN's, and in fact most countries in the world's, conceptual basis for resolving the conflict.

Abba Eban. The Israeli minister of foreign affairs.

The Arab "No"

Representatives of the Arab states convened several weeks after the war in Khartoum, Sudan, to discuss the unfavorable outcomes of the war for them. They announced the three familiar "no"s that summarized their determination to continue with violent struggle:

1. No to recognizing Israel.

2. No to negotiations with Israel.

3. No to peace with Israel.

We now know that Egypt and Jordan eventually decided to sign peace treaties with Israel. However, in the first few years after the Six Day War, all the Arab countries continued their hostility.

Rapid Rehabilitation of the Arab Armies. Continued Low-Intensity Hostilities.

Both Egypt and Syria, whose armies completely fell apart in the war, immediately turned to the Soviet Union for assistance. The acute need to rehabilitate the army overrode any other consideration. The army was necessary for Syria, Jordan, and Egypt not only to continue the struggle with Israel, but to ensure the regime's survival. The Soviet arms factories sent enormous quantities of weapons to the Egyptians and Syrians. Relying on recruits from their large population, the two countries built new military frameworks within a few months. Within a year and a half, their armies already returned to their pre-war prowess. Then they continued to get numerically and technologically stronger. The military buildup began to restore some self-confidence to the Arab states, and clashes along the ceasefire lines began to break out (the first clash as early as July 1, 1967 on the Suez Canal). This violent period was later called the War of Attrition, in which Nasser sought to drain Israel's blood. This was done with the help of Syria and Jordan and the PLO's sabotage and terrorist activities.

More than 1,000 Israelis (more than the losses in the Six Day War), 10,000 Egyptians, hundreds of Syrians, hundreds of Jordanians and PLO members, and dozens of Soviet "advisers" were killed. This war ended in a ceasefire in August 1970. It was a non-decisive ending without any territorial change. Shortly thereafter, ill and exhausted, Gamal Abdel Nasser died. Millions attended the funeral. It has been said about the famous leader that in a way, the man already died on June 5, 1967. Although he survived the staggering defeat of the Six Day War, Nasser was unable to recover from it.

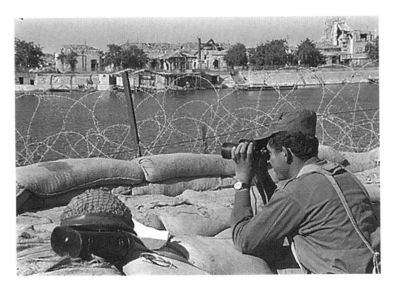

IDF soldiers scouts the Egyptian side of the Suez canal 1970.
(Picture by Milner Moshe)

After the Six Day War, there were more political upheavals and power struggles in Syria. Despite the disgraceful failure of the Syrian Air Force commander in 1967, Hafez al-Assad, he managed to continue advancing and establishing his control of the army. In November 1970, he staged a military coup and ruthlessly eliminated his opponents to become a new dictator. From then and until the civil war in Syria broke out, the Assad family ruled Syria with unabashed force and brutality.

Jordan Withdraws from the War

Jordan lost the most important territories in the war - Judea and Samaria, including East Jerusalem. The Jordanian

King's image was seriously damaged. But he managed to stay in power. Due to the fact that Israel took over the entire West Bank, the Palestinian organizations moved to work against Israel from the eastern bank of the river - that is, from the Kingdom of Jordan. Between 1967 and 1970, these organizations carried out hundreds of attacks on Israel, with the help of the Jordanian army and the Arab states. The IDF reacted forcefully to the PLO and the Jordanian army. The internal instability in Jordan culminated in a PLO rebellion in September 1970. The Palestinians were supported by Syrian invasion to northern Jordan. Although the King's Arab Legion defeated them, it did so with the help of the United States, which recruited Israel for this purpose. Under threat of concentrating IDF forces on the Golan Heights, the Syrians retreated and the King was free to crush the PLO. At least 10,000 people were killed or massacred. After "Black September", as this period of fighting was called, Jordan withdrew from the cycle of fighting in Israel (with the exception of symbolic participation in the Yom Kippur War in Syria). Although an official peace treaty was signed only in 1994, in practice the Jordanian-Israeli border has been quiet since 1970, with very few incidents. The PLO, which was defeated in Jordan, transferred its hostile activity to Lebanon under Syria's patronage. Lebanon's relative stability soon began to crumble and the country collapsed into a terrible civil war.

CHAPTER 8:

The Great Rift

Jewish settlement in the territories

As early as the summer of 1967, a Plan was published by Maj. Gen. (res.) and Minister Yigal Allon. The plan proposed security settlement in areas of the West Bank, southern Gaza Strip, and several areas in the Sinai. Allon sought to disperse the fog around the fate of the occupied territories. According to the plan, areas would be annexed mainly in sparsely populated or empty areas in the eastern West Bank. The rest of the territory, populated by Arabs, would be returned to Jordan or become autonomous according to a referendum of its inhabitants. The Allon plan was never officially accepted, but it was the base for building settlements in the territories in the decade following the Six Day War. Only neighborhoods in East

Jerusalem and the Old City were annexed. The Arab inhabitants were given permanent resident status in Israel and Jewish neighborhoods were built on the annexed lands.

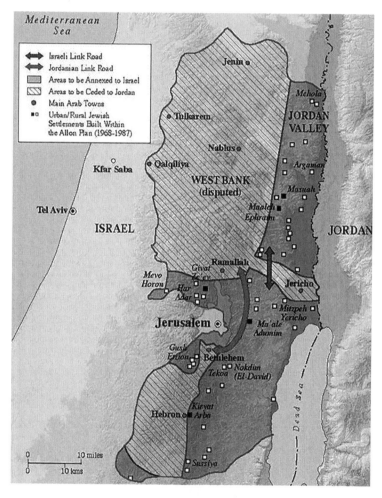

The Map of Allon plan

Since the mid-1970s, religious Zionism has taken the lead in building the settlements. The settlements are no longer only for permanent presence for security purposes. Settlers now moved to the territories on religious ideological grounds. In 1977, a right-wing government came to power for the first time in Israel and began a period in which the trend of Jewish settlement in the territories expanded, even in Arab-populated areas.

Since the mid-1980s, all Israeli governments have not approved the construction of many new settlements. The unwillingness to declare full annexation of all the territories, including right-wing governments, is the reason for this conduct. Greater annexation of Judea and Samaria will force Israel, under tremendous pressure, to grant citizenship to the masses of Palestinians living there. This will endanger the requisite Jewish majority for the Jewish state. Alternatively, annexing the territory while leaving the Palestinians without rights like the rest of Israel's citizens would turn Israel to an undemocratic apartheid state. In other words: in the event of annexation, Jewish democracy will have to give up one of its basic elements: either democracy or Jewish identity.

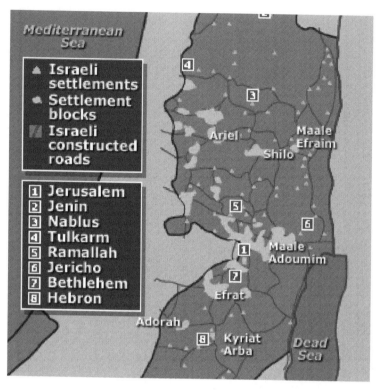

Map of the Israeli settlements in the West Bank

In fact, since the early 1980s, most of the Jewish construction carried out under the orders of the Israeli governments was only for the expansion of existing settlements. Most of the new settlements that have been built in the territories over the past 20 years began as illegal outposts. Some of them were retroactively recognized as legal, some of them forcibly evicted, and some are still illegal.

Jewish Settlement in the Golan

A small group of settlers had already moved to the Golan Heights in July 1967, and settled in an abandoned Syrian base. This group received temporary approval from the army and later became a recognized community. Additional groups went to the Golan shortly thereafter. The new Jewish towns that became permanent points served as an anchor for presence in the area. A combination of security and value-driven settlement characterizes Israeli policy and, in fact, the Zionist movement since its establishment. In 1981, Israeli Prime Minister Menachem Begin led a process of formally annexing the Golan Heights to Israel. Since then, Israeli Law applies to the Golan Heights, but the rest of the world considers it, at least officially, as an occupied territory.

Settlement in the Gaza Area and Northern Sinai

In the 1970s, Jewish settlement also began in the Gaza Strip and northern Sinai. The towns in the densely populated Gaza Strip were mostly concentrated to the south. The settlers made their living from advanced greenhouse agriculture developed in the sand dunes. To the south, in the northwestern Sinai, other settlements were built and their urban center was the town of Yamit. The settlements in Sinai did not last long and all were evacuated and destroyed before Sinai was returned to Egypt in 1981, as part of the peace treaty.

The Gaza Strip settlements existed until 2005 when Israel withdrew from the Gaza Strip. Despite widespread support and protest, Ariel Sharon, who was Prime Minister at the time, decided to fully evacuate all these settlements.

The disengagement from Gaza 2005. Fortified on the roof, settlers from Kfar Darom pouring oil on the police officers. (Picture taken by Milner Moshe).

The Great rift inside Israel

Without a doubt, one of the long-term effects of the Six Day War is on the political and social debate in Israel. Levi Eshkol's many efforts to prevent the war proved to many countries that Israel was not the aggressor. The results of these efforts were that the world did not rush to pressure withdrawal from the occupied territories, like it did after the Sinai War in 1956. In addition, the Arabs' total refusal to enter into negotiations with Israel after the war gave it additional legitimacy to continue holding on to the territories. There is no doubt, however, that the continued Israeli presence in the territories - particularly in Judea and Samaria - is causing intense debate within Israeli society and beyond. Despite the long peace process with the Palestinians the fate of the territories is still undecided.

The question of the legitimacy of Jewish settlement in the territories is pending. This is a difficult political and ethical question to which there is no unequivocal answer. Continued direct or indirect Israeli control of millions of Palestinians is a very difficult issue. If we try to sum up the great debate between the Israeli Right and the Center-Left, we can summarize each side's arguments as follows:

The Israeli Right sees Judea and Samaria as legitimate territory of the Jewish state. Land from which the Jewish nation was born and which belongs to it by virtue of history. According to this logic, these are not occupied territories at all, but areas of a homeland that were liberated in a defensive war. Moreover, the Right Wing stresses the supreme security need of a continued Israeli presence in Judea and Samaria, which constitute a critical mountainous area for the protection of Jerusalem and the coastal plain.

Rabbi Zvi Yehuda Kook, one of the leaders of religious Zionism, said the following in a conversation with Moshe Dayan after the Six Day War:

"There are no Arab areas or lands here, but the lands of Israel, eternal ancestral patrimony, on which others came and built without our permission in our absence. We never abandoned or alienated ourselves from the patrimony of our forefathers (...) it is thus incumbent upon us to liberate the lands."

The Israeli Left looks at the Arabs living in the territories and sees a people placed under military occupation and living without full human rights. According to this logic, continuing the occupation is unethical and Israeli democracy must not continue with it. Furthermore, the Left stresses the danger of losing the Jewish majority needed by the State of Israel or alternatively the danger of becoming an apartheid state - which the world will not tolerate.

Here is an excerpt from Professor Yeshayahu Leibowitz's letter to Moshe Dayan after the war:

"...The predicament of the "Territories" doesn't interest me at all. What concerns me is the 1.25 million Arabs living there, not for concern of them but rather out of concern for the Jewish people and our nation. Inclusion of these Arabs (in addition to the 300,000 already living in the state) under our rule – means the destruction of Israel as a Jewish state; the annihilation of the entire Jewish nation and ruin of the society and social framework that we established in our country".

I took this picture in Jerusalem of June 2017. The man holding an Israeli flag is also holding a sign with right wing massages of Jewish rights on the land. He confronts people from a left wing demonstration, calling for two state solutions – which mean an Israeli retreat from the West Bank.

The Six Day War ended fifty years ago, but its echoes still reverberate today. The State of Israel is in a tough position with regards to the territories it gained in the brief war.

The huge victory has become Israel's greatest challenge and the biggest question looming over its future.

Bibliography

אורן. ר. (2004). *המטרה: תל אביב.* תל אביב: קשת.

אל סכאכיני. ח. (2007). *כזה הוא אני רבותיי.* תל אביב: צבעונים.

ארליך. ח. (2017). *המזרח התיכון - המשבר הגדול ביותר מאז מוחמד.* ראשון לציון: ידיעות ספרים

בן מאיר. ד. (1994). *יצחק רבין.* תל אביב: אביבים.

גביש. י. (2016). *סדין אדום.* אור יהודה: כינרת זמורה ביתן.

גלבר. י. (2004). *קוממיות ונכבה.* תל אביב: דביר.

דינור. ב. צ. (1958). *תולדות ההגנה.* תל אביב: עם עובד.

הרכבי. י. (1992). *מלחמה ואסטרטגיה.* תל אביב: משרד הביטחון.

ויצטום. א. קליאן. מ. (2013). *ירושלים של קדושה ושיגעון.* רמות השבים: אריה ניר

חפר. ח. טל. ש. (1988). *יגאל.* כפר תבור: הקיבוץ המאוחד.

חפר. ח. ינקו. מ. (1968). *מסדר הלוחמים.* תל אביב: עמיקם

מוריס. ב. (2003). *קורבנות: תולדות הסכסוך הציוני-ערבי 1881-2001*. תל אביב: ספריית אופקים.

נרקיס. ע. (1993). *אחת ירושלים*. תל אביב: הדפסת המחבר.

סופר א. (2006). *המאבק על המים במזרח התיכון*. תל אביב: עם עובד.

שפירא. א. (2015). *בן גוריון, דמותו של מנהיג*. תל אביב: עם עובד.

Collins. L. Lapierre D. (1988). USA: Simone and Schuster.

Deighton. L. (1986). *Blitzkrieg.* Israel: Ministry of Defense.

Teveth. S. (1968). *The tanks of Tammuz. USA: Weidenfeld & Nicolson.*

Lewis, B. (1993). *The Arabs in history.* England. Oxford university press.

Oren. M. B. (2003). *Six days of war.* USA: The random house publishing group

Perrett. B. (1991). *The last stand!.* USA addition: Cassell military paperbacks

Peres. S. (1993). *The new middle east.* Bnai-Brak: Stimatzki.

Pressfield. S. (2014). *The lions gate.* USA: nine sisters imports Inc.

Shavit. A. (2013). *My promised land.* New York:Shpiegel and Grau.

Simhoni. S. (1968). *The great victory in pictures.* Tel Aviv: Ester.

The pictures and the maps in this book where taken from:

Government press office (Israel)
The National Photo collection (Israel)
https://www.wikipedia.org/
The IDF Archive
My own photos

About the writer:

Amit Grinfeld is a licensed tour guide in Israel, with 10 years of experience. He has a BA degree in history and international relations from the Hebrew University of Jerusalem and an MA degree in Public Policy from Tel Aviv University. Amit has guided hundreds of groups including youth, Birthright, family tours, Christian pilgrims, VIP visitors in Israel, official guests of the Ministry of Foreign Affairs, Donors of the JNF, Journalists, press, army and police units and more. Most recently Amit has been invited to lecture on "The Six Day War - 50 Years Later" in communities throughout the United States. Amit is married and is a father of 2 young children. He serves in the IDF as a Staff Major in the home front command.

51603755R00066

Made in the USA
Lexington, KY
12 September 2019